THE WOW AND THE HOW

DINOSAURS

SUSIE WILLIAMS

Gareth Stevens PUBLISHING

Please visit our website, www.garethstevens.com. For a free color catalog of all our high-quality books, call toll free 1-800-542-2595 or fax 1-877-542-2596.

Cataloging-in-Publication Data
Names: Williams, Susie.
Title: Dinosaurs / Susie Williams.
Description: Buffalo, NY : Gareth Stevens Publishing, 2026. | Series: The wow and the how | Includes glossary and index.
Identifiers: ISBN 9781482473063 (pbk.) | ISBN 9781482473070 (library bound) | ISBN 9781482473087 (ebook)
Subjects: LCSH: Dinosaurs--Juvenile literature.
Classification: LCC QE861.5 W555 2026 | DDC 567.9--dc23

Published in 2026 by
Gareth Stevens Publishing
2544 Clinton St.
Buffalo, NY 14224

First published in Great Britain in 2024 by Hodder & Stoughton

Authors: Paul Rockett, Victoria Brooker, Sarah Peutrill, Julia Bird, Grace Glendinning, Jenni Lazell

Consultant: Dr David Hone, Reader at Queen Mary University, London

Series designer: Rocket Design (East Anglia) Ltd

Picture credits:
Alamy: MasPix 8-9.
Science Photo Library: Carlton Publishing Group 16b.
Shutterstock: Alexonline 25c; AmeliAU 6-7; Caron Badkin 11br; Tom Bangkeaw 27c; Bee_acg 17c; BlueRingMedia 19br; Catmando 14-15; Alex Coan 10b; David Costa art 4-5; DM7 4b, 28l; Dotted Yeti 27c; Elenarts 12-13; Elena Elisseeva 28-29; Emi 16c; Daniel Eskridge 20-21, 22-23; GraficRF.com 18-19c; Marija Ivancic 11c; Kagera 29br; Kitty Vector 3t, 5bl,16tl, 16tr, 17cr, 17cl, 17cr; Kataryna Lanskaya 13c; Ron Leishman 29cr; Julia Matvi 18-19; MikhailSh 29cl; Mopic 13b; Dmitry Natashin 7c; Newelle 10c; NotionPic 5br, 23br; PitubeART 27b; Sabelskaya 31tr; Yuliia Sonsedska 25b; Spiro 24-25; Sudowoodo 21br; Tinkivinki 6bl; Uiliaaa 15t; Hedzun Vasyl front cover, 1; Vector Radiance 16-17; Vector Tradition 2; Warpaint 10-11; White Space Illustrations 17b; YG Studio 7bl; Zaleman 6br; Alyona Zhitnaya 3bl, 5tr, 9bl.
Wikimedia: Paleopod CCA-A 4.0 International 23c.

All additional design elements from Shutterstock or drawn by designer.

Printed in the United States of America

CPSIA compliance information: Batch #CSGS26: For further information contact Gareth Stevens at 1-800-542-2595.

CONTENTS

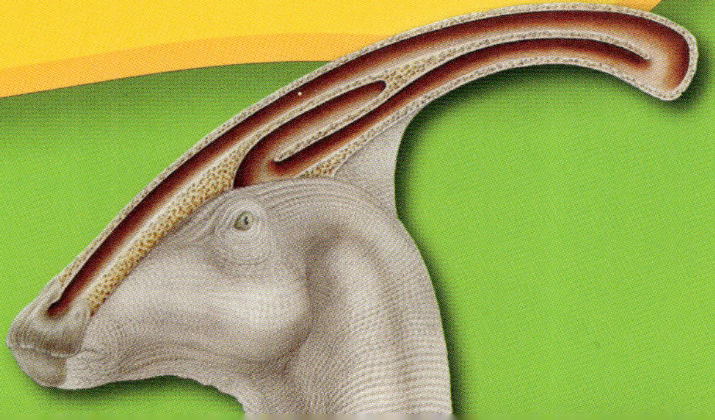

THE WOW OF DINOSAURS!

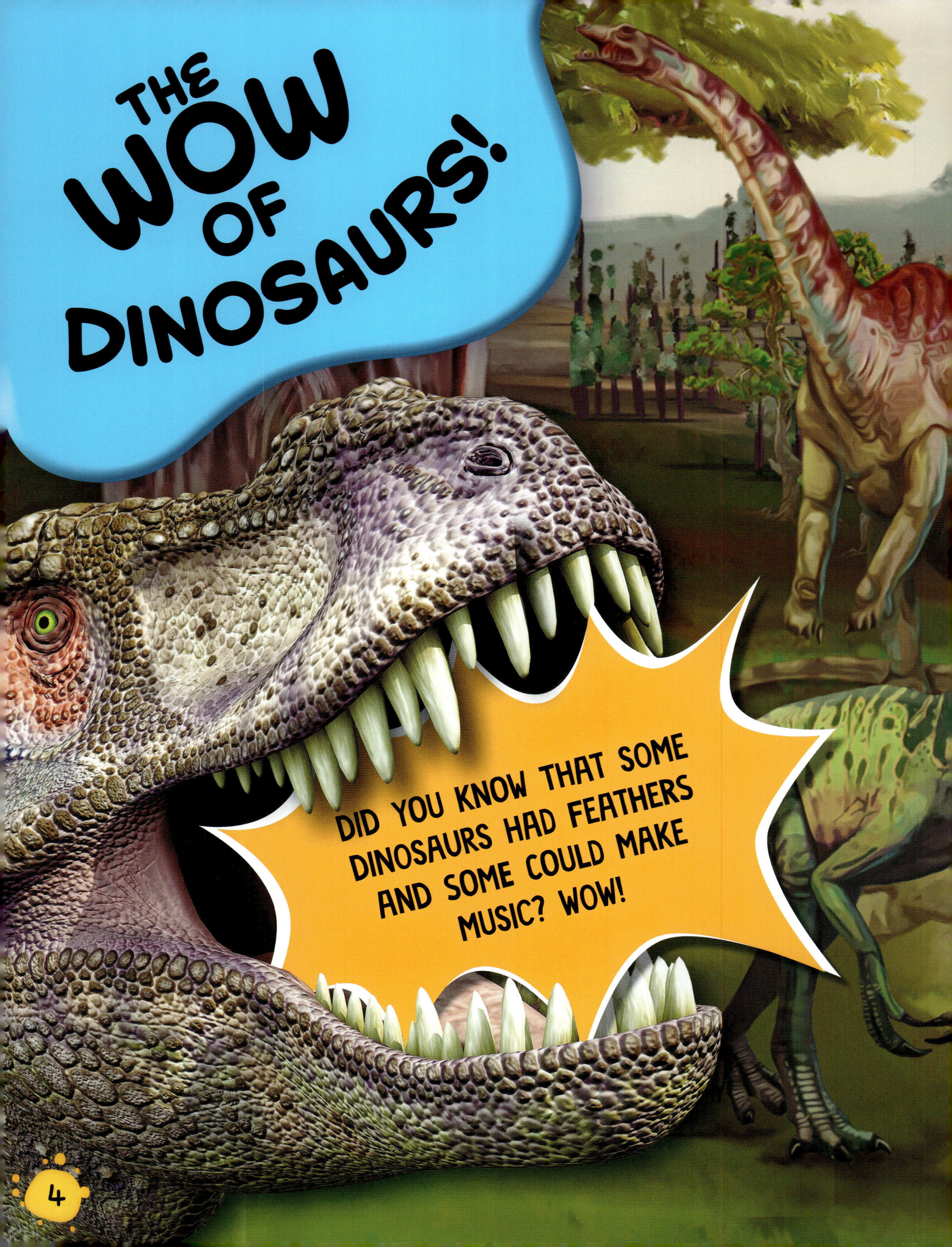

DID YOU KNOW THAT SOME DINOSAURS HAD FEATHERS AND SOME COULD MAKE MUSIC? WOW!

We know about dinosaurs because of **HOW** scientists, called paleontologists, work. Paleontologists spend a lot of time at prehistoric sites looking for fossils. Fossils are the remains of plants and animals that lived long ago.

Each fossil is carefully removed, cleaned, and studied. From studying fossils, paleontologists build up a picture of what each dinosaur might have looked like. We now know that some dinosaurs had over 1,000 teeth, some had tiny brains and one had the strongest bite of any land animal ever!

Read more amazing facts about dinosaurs, including some that may challenge what you thought you knew. Find the science behind the facts to understand more about dinosaurs and how they lived. Can you find your own **WOW** facts too?

WOW!

Some Triassic dinos were extinct before Cretaceous dinos existed!

DINOSAURS LIVED ON EARTH FOR MILLIONS OF YEARS.

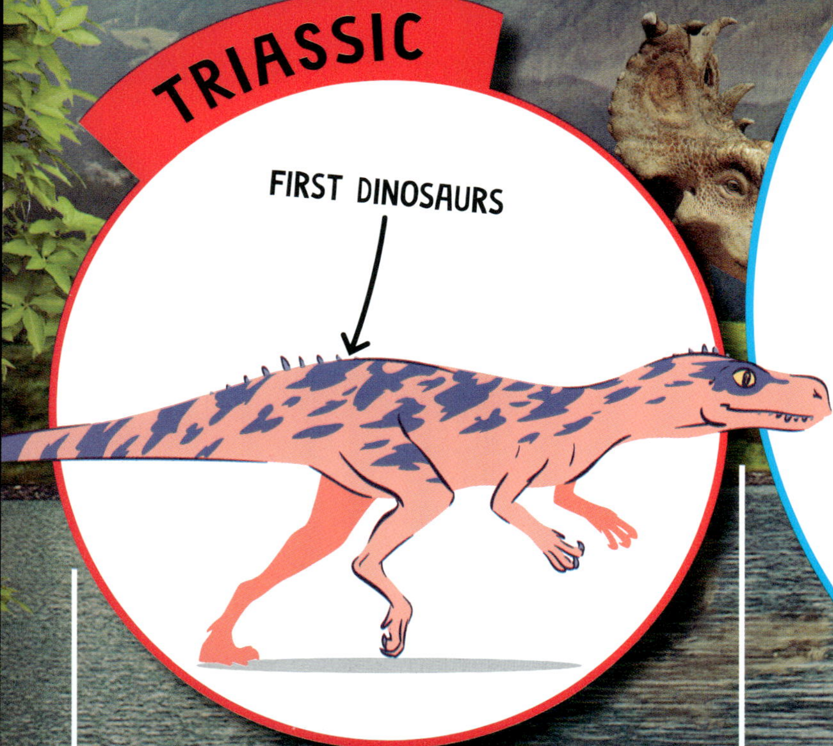

252

201

MILLION YEARS AGO

HOW?

Dinosaurs roamed the planet for around 165 million years! Over such a long period of time, dinosaurs evolved. This means they changed into different types, or species. Few species lived longer than a few million years.

The age of dinosaurs is split into three time periods: the Triassic, the Jurassic, and the Cretaceous. Different species of dinosaur didn't all exist for this whole time. Some species were separated by millions of years!

AMAZING DINOSAURS

Compared to the length of time that dinosaurs roamed Earth, humans have been here for just a blink of the eye—a short 300,000 years!

WOW!

A fossil exists of dinosaurs fighting to the death!

TWO UNLUCKY DINOSAURS HAVE BEEN PRESERVED FOREVER, LOCKED IN A **FIERCE FIGHT.**

HOW?

Fossils are usually formed when an animal dies and is buried in sediment like mud or sand. The soft parts of its body rot away, but when conditions are right, over millions of years, the hard parts like the bones and teeth actually become part of the rock and are known as a fossil. This is what happened to two dinosaurs, a *Velociraptor* and a *Protoceratops*, around 67 million years ago.

From their fossil, discovered in Mongolia in 1971, scientists have worked out that the *Velociraptor* struck the *Protoceratops* in the neck with its sharp claws and the *Protoceratops* bit the *Velociraptor's* arm. Sadly, neither dinosaur survived the encounter. A nearby sand bank collapsed, burying them both.

AMAZING DINOSAURS

There are some fossils that show how a dinosaur lived rather than how they looked. These are called trace fossils. They are records of a dinosaur's activity, rather than part of the dinosaur itself. Trace fossils of footprints, burrows, and even poop have been found!

WOW!

Huge dinosaurs did huge poops!

Look out below!

WE KNOW ABOUT DINOSAUR DROPPINGS BECAUSE SOME OF THE POOP BECAME FOSSILS CALLED COPROLITES. THE BIGGEST COPROLITE EVER FOUND WAS ABOUT THE SIZE OF TWO FOOTBALLS SIDE-BY-SIDE!

The size of a typical human poop ...

... compared to a monster dino coprolite!

HOW?

Coprolites are astonishing feats of nature, as poop usually breaks down quite quickly after it leaves the body. But with just the right conditions, some high pressure and lots of time, poop and everything inside it can be explored millions of years later.

Scientists use the size, shape, and contents of the poop to learn a lot about the dinosaur it came from: was it a plant eater, fish eater, or meat eater (or all three)? What shape were its intestines, how did it bite and chew, and where did it roam?

Coprolites come in many shapes, colors, and sizes.

AMAZING DINOSAURS

The first person to break into a coprolite and explore the insides was Mary Anning (1799–1847).

WOW!

You drink the same water as the dinosaurs!

WATER HAS BEEN AROUND FOR NEARLY FIVE BILLION YEARS AND WOULD HAVE BEEN DRUNK BY THIRSTY DINOSAURS!

HOW?

Water first found its way to Earth billions of years ago when icy comets and asteroids from space crashed into its surface. Over time, rivers, lakes, and oceans formed. From their surface, warm droplets of water turned into vapor and traveled up into the air where they cooled again to became water, forming clouds.

Eventually the clouds became too heavy and the water fell back to Earth as rain or snow, refilling Earth's waterways. And the cycle began all over again! This is called the water cycle and it is essential for the survival of all animals on Earth, including the dinosaurs.

AMAZING DINOSAURS

The asteroids and comets that brought water to Earth also caused the extinction of the dinosaurs. Around 66 million years, a huge asteroid struck Earth, killing off the dinosaurs and many other animals.

WOW!

Duck-billed dinosaurs made music!

PALEONTOLOGISTS THINK A GROUP OF DUCK-BILLED DINOSAURS, OR HADROSAURS, COULD PRODUCE A LOW SOUND FROM THE LARGE, TRUMPET-LIKE CREST ON THEIR HEAD TO COMMUNICATE WITH EACH OTHER.

HOW?

Paleontologists studied fossils to discover that the long, bony crest of the *Parasaurolophus* was a hollow tube, connected to its nostrils. When the dinosaur pushed air through the tube, its crest may have made its honking calls louder, like a built-in speaker. People think the calls would have sounded a bit like a foghorn—or a massive trombone!

AMAZING DINOSAURS

Various dinosaurs had features like bony plates. Others had fleshy combs like a rooster. But not all could make music!

WOW!

Dinosaurs came in all kinds of colors!

DINOSAURS COULD HAVE BEEN SHADES OF RED, YELLOW, AND BLUE!

HOW?

Scientists have discovered teeny tiny structures inside dinosaur fossils called melanosomes. These contained color molecules. Scientists study these melanosomes and compare them to those found in modern animals to give us their best guess of what colors dinosaurs could have been.

Anchiornis looked a bit like a magpie with a red crest, while *Sinosauropteryx* had a stripy tail and a mask on its face like a racoon.

AMAZING DINOSAURS

There may have even been some dinosaurs with shimmering hummingbird colors.

WOW! All dinosaurs could swim!

LARGE DINOSAURS LOOK LIKE THEY WOULD SINK IN WATER, BUT EVEN THE MASSIVE *T. REX* MIGHT TAKE A DIP.

HOW?

Dinosaurs would swim to find food or cool off. They could swim to cross a river or to reach an island.

Like all reptiles, dinosaurs needed to breathe air so they would keep their heads above water. Some dinosaurs, such as *Spinosaurus* and *Baryonyx*, had heads like crocodiles. There were other reptiles and amphibians alive at the same time as dinosaurs and some of these lived mainly in the sea.

AMAZING DINOSAURS

Spinosaurus had a nostril on the side of its snout. This meant it could still breathe when part of its head was underwater while feeding.

WOW!

Human brains weigh more than dinosaur brains!

AN AVERAGE HUMAN BRAIN WEIGHS ABOUT 2.8 POUNDS (1.3 KG) WHILE THE BRAIN OF *DIPLODOCUS* WEIGHED ONLY 0.22 POUND (0.1 KG) (THE SAME AS A TENNIS BALL).

HOW?

Despite its massive body–weighing in around 177 times more than a human–*Diplodocus* had a very small head compared to its body. Its brain was small and light.

Diplodocus was so big that it had no natural predators. As a herbivore, mainly eating leaves, it had plenty of food. So, with little to bother its easy life, *Diplodocus* had no need for a big brain. Humans, on the other hand, evolved with more complex needs and challenges to face in order to survive. Bigger, more intelligent brains helped us meet these needs.

AMAZING DINOSAURS

Troodon may have been a smarter dinosaur than most, as it had a brain that was bigger than we'd expect for the size of its body.

I don't bother with a dentist ... I can just replace my rotten teeth!

WOW!

Hadrosaurs could have over 1,000 teeth!

HADROSAURS WERE PLANT EATERS THAT EVOLVED WITH SOME PRETTY AMAZING TEETH!

HOW?

Hadrosaurs are a mostly late Cretaceous group of dinosaurs known for their long beaks. Hadrosaurs were impressive chewing machines. A hadrosaur's mouth had closely spaced teeth stacked in rows in its jaws. As the teeth at the top wore down, new ones grew up from the bottom.

Hadrosaurs' rows of teeth were able to chew to mush the toughest plant matter, such as leaves, twigs, and even conifer needles.

An adult and a young (front right) hadrosaur jawbone.

AMAZING DINOSAURS

Hadrosaurs lost about 1,800 teeth a year, leaving behind plenty of fossils for paleontologists to find and study!

WOW! Chickens are dinosaurs!

ALL BIRDS EVOLVED FROM SMALL, MEAT EATING DINOSAURS—SO EVERY BIRD IS A LIVING DINOSAUR!

HOW?

The group of dinosaurs that includes today's birds is called maniraptora. Birds are very different in many ways to others in this group, but all maniraptorans are united by some special features, including:

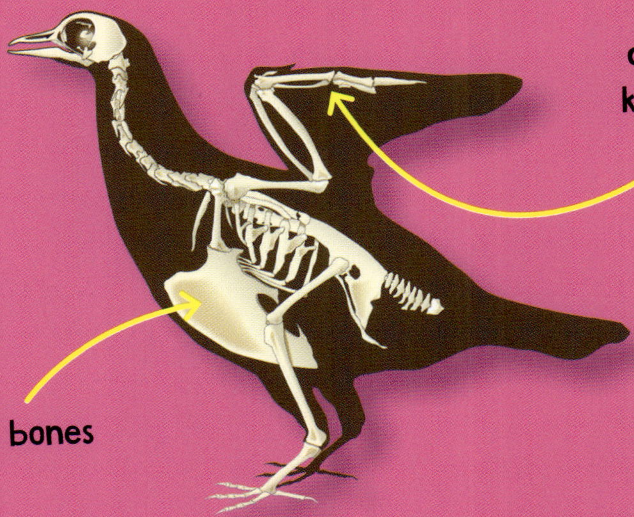

Maniraptorans are the only group that includes flying dinosaurs, and has members that were fully feathered, not just a little bit feathered.

AMAZING DINOSAURS

Some non-bird maniraptorans had brains ready to fly. Just like birds' brains, theirs were much larger at the front to give excellent vision and coordination.

WOW!

All dinosaurs walked on tiptoe!

DINOSAURS AREN'T THE ONLY ANIMALS TO TIPTOE AROUND. MANY ANIMALS, INCLUDING DOGS, CATS, AND CHICKENS, ALSO WALK ON THEIR TOES!

HOW?

Fossils show that most dinosaurs didn't flatten their feet like humans do. Almost all dinosaurs walked on their toes, with their heels off the ground. The scientific term for this is digitigrady.

Dinosaurs had long feet and strong toes. Walking on tiptoe made them faster, which was important for hunting prey or escaping from predators.

AMAZING DINOSAURS

Large sauropods had a soft pad on their heels. This was like having cushions on their feet to help support their enormous weight.

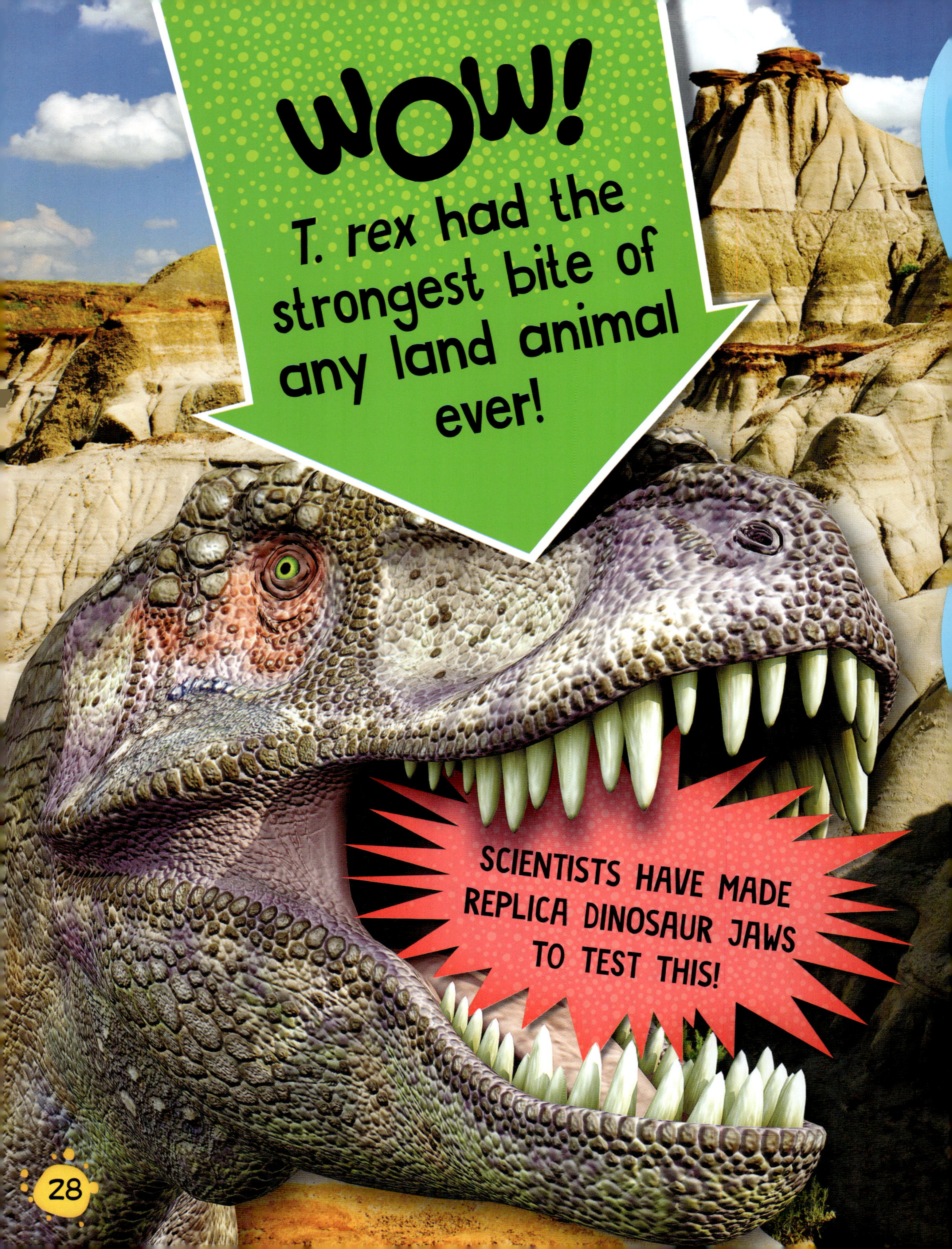

WOW!

T. rex had the strongest bite of any land animal ever!

SCIENTISTS HAVE MADE REPLICA DINOSAUR JAWS TO TEST THIS!

How?

When an animal bites, the muscles in the head pull on the jaw to close it. How hard an animal can bite depends on the size of the jaw and the muscles–the bigger, the better!

The enormous *T. rex* had a huge mouth full of teeth and superstrong jaw muscles. This combination gave it the strongest bite of any land animal. Researchers figured out that its bite was 10 times stronger than an alligator's!

AMAZING DINOSAURS

T-rex had a mouth full of 60 teeth, some of which were 6 inches (15 cm) long. Watch out!

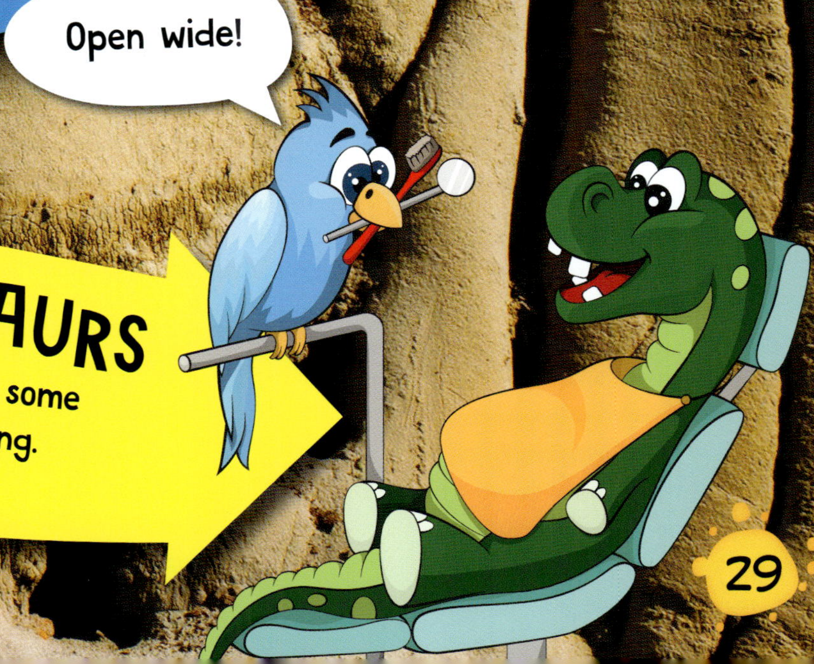

GLOSSARY

asteroid small rocky object that moves around the sun

coordination the ability to move around carefully and effectively

extinct no longer existing

evolve how a species (such as a type of dinosaur) changes over a long time

herbivorve an animal that only eats plants

intestines long tubes that are part of an animal's digestive system

predator an animal that hunts other animals for food.

prey an animal that is hunted or caught for food, usually by another animal.

replica a copy of something

vapor a liquid that has become a gas because of heat

FURTHER READING

BOOKS

Cats React to Dinosaur Facts
by Izzi Howell (Wayland, 2022)

Fact or Fake: The Truth about Dinosaurs
by Sonya Newland (Wayland, 2022)

Whose Bum did *T-Rex* Bite? (Dinosaur Science series)
By Dr. Dave Hone (Wayland, 2023)

WEBSITES

www.nhm.ac.uk/discover/dinosaurs.html
Everything you ever wanted to know about dinosaurs!

www.natgeokids.com/uk/play-and-win/games/dinosaur-memory/
Do a fun dinosaur quiz

https://australian.museum/learn/dinosaurs/dinosaurs-on-the-attack/
Learn about how dinosaurs attacked as well as other interesting facts

INDEX